50 FRENCH PHRASES

Catherine Bruzzone and Susan Martineau

Illustrations by Leighton Noyes
French adviser: Marie-Thérèse Bougard

Contents

Special note for learners!

The key French phrases you will learn are numbered on each spread. There are also extra words you will need for the activities. By the end of the book you will know 50 FRENCH PHRASES and lots of useful French words. There is a summary of all these at the back of the book.

Pronouncing French

The simple pronunciation guide will help but it cannot be completely accurate. Read the words as naturally as possible as if they were English. Put the stress on the letters in *italics*, e.g. boh-*shoor*. Don't roll the 'r' at the end of a word, e.g. 'ler', French for 'the'. Ask for help from a French-speaking person and try to speak without the guide as soon as you can.

Bonjour!

Have some fun saying hello and goodbye in French. You need to match the right greeting to the pictures, according to the time of day illustrated. Say the correct phrase out loud. You can check your answers on page 32.

1

Bonjour
boh-*shoor*
Hello,
good morning

2

Au revoir
oh r'v*wahr*
Goodbye

3

Bonsoir
boh-*swahr*
Good evening

4

Bonne nuit
bon nwee
Goodnight

Words to Know

Salut!
sal*oo*
Hi!

À bientôt
ah bee-an-*toh*
See you soon

le jour
ler shoor
day

le soir
ler swahr
evening

la nuit
la nwee
night

Je m'appelle...

Ask your friends or family to play this naming game with you. One person needs to be blindfolded and twirled round. They then have to 'find' someone and ask **Comment tu t'appelles?** The person answers **Je m'appelle...** and says **Et toi?** Take it in turns to be the 'finder'. You could all choose a French name!

5

Comment tu t'appelles?
kom-oh too ta*pell*
What's your name?

6

Je m'appelle...
sh' ma*pell*...
My name is...

7

Et toi?
eh twah
And you?

Choose a Name!

Alexandre
alex-*ahn*-dr

Nicolas
nee-kol-*ah*

Antoine
ahn-*twahn*

Thomas
toe-*mah*

Marie
ma-*ree*

Camille
kam-*eel*

Sarah
sah-*rah*

Manon
ma-*noh*

Quel âge as-tu?

You will need two dice for this game. One person throws them and the other asks **Quel âge as-tu?**
The dice thrower answers **J'ai... ans**, putting in the number the dice add up to. Take it in turns.

8

Quel âge as-tu?
kell ah-sh ah-too
How old are you?

9

J'ai neuf ans
shay nerf ahn
I am nine years old

10

Bon anniversaire!
bon-anni-vair*sair*
Happy birthday!

Numbers! Numbers!

1	**un**	ahn		**7**	**sept**	set
2	**deux**	der		**8**	**huit**	weet
3	**trois**	trwah		**9**	**neuf**	nerf
4	**quatre**	katr'		**10**	**dix**	deess
5	**cinq**	sank		**11**	**onze**	onz
6	**six**	seess		**12**	**douze**	dooz

Look at the numbers on the inside front cover if you want to ask some older people their ages!

Ça va?

Cut out a circle of paper or card. Draw a smiley face on one side and a sad one on the other. Ask a friend **Ça va?** as you show them one of the faces. They have to try and give the right answer depending on if it is smiley or glum. Swap round so that you can practise too.

11

Ça va?
sa-vah
How are you?

12

Ça va bien, merci
sa-vah bee-ah mair-see
I'm fine, thanks

13

Ça ne va pas bien
sa ner vah *pah bee*-ah
I'm not so well

Words to Know

Affreux
ah-fre*r*
Awful

Assez bien
ah-*seh bee*-ah
Quite well

Comme ci comme ça
kom *see* kom *sa*
So-so

Très bien
tr*eh bee*-ah
Very good

Merci
mair-*see*
Thank you/thanks

Où est...?

Find all of the items in the **Words to Know** list and put them
on a tray. Practise saying the French words for them. Now
close your eyes while a friend takes one item off the tray.
(Cover up the French words too.) You then have to ask
Où est le/la...? whatever the missing thing is!
Your friend will either say **Voilà le/la...** or
Encore une fois! Take it in turns
to have a go at remembering.

14

Où est...?
oo eh
Where is,..?

15

Voilà le/la,...
vwah-lah ler/lah
Here is the,..

Encore une fois!
on-kor yoon *fwah*
Try again!

A Note About Le and La
There are two words for 'the' in French – **le** and **la**.
Try to learn them when you learn a new noun.

Words to Know

le livre
ler leevr'
book

le crayon
ler cray-*oh*
pencil

le crayon de couleur
ler cray-*oh* der cool-*err*
colour pencil

la colle
lah koll
glue

le papier
ler papee-*eh*
paper

le stylo
ler steel*o*
pen

la gomme
lah gom
rubber

la règle
lah ray-gl'
ruler

Qu'est-ce que c'est?

Look at this outdoor scene and practise saying the French words. Then ask some friends or your family to play a drawing game with you. You each take it in turns to draw one of the named items and ask **Qu'est-ce-que c'est?** Everyone else has to try and say what it is from the drawing (and without looking at the French words). They say **C'est un/une….**

17

Qu'est-ce que c'est?
kesker seh
What is it?

une fille
oon fee
girl

un vélo
ahn *vaylo*
bicycle

un pique-nique
ahn peek-*neek*
picnic

12

un oiseau
ahn nwas-*o*
bird

un ballon
ahn ball*oh*
ball

18

C'est un/une...
set ahn/oon
It's a...

un sac à dos
ahn sak ah doh
backpack

un banc
ahn boh
bench

un garçon
ahn gar-*soh*
boy

A Note About Un and Une
There are two words for 'a' in French – **un** and **une**.
You say **C'est un** for a **le** word and **C'est une** for a
la word. For example, **C'est une fille** or **C'est un banc.**

Voici la famille

Spot the family! Look at page 15. Which four people are members of the same family? Point them out and say **Voici le fils** or **Voici la fille**. Use other words from **Words to Know** with **Voici** too. When you have found the whole family, you can say **Voici la famille**. Check your answers on page 32.

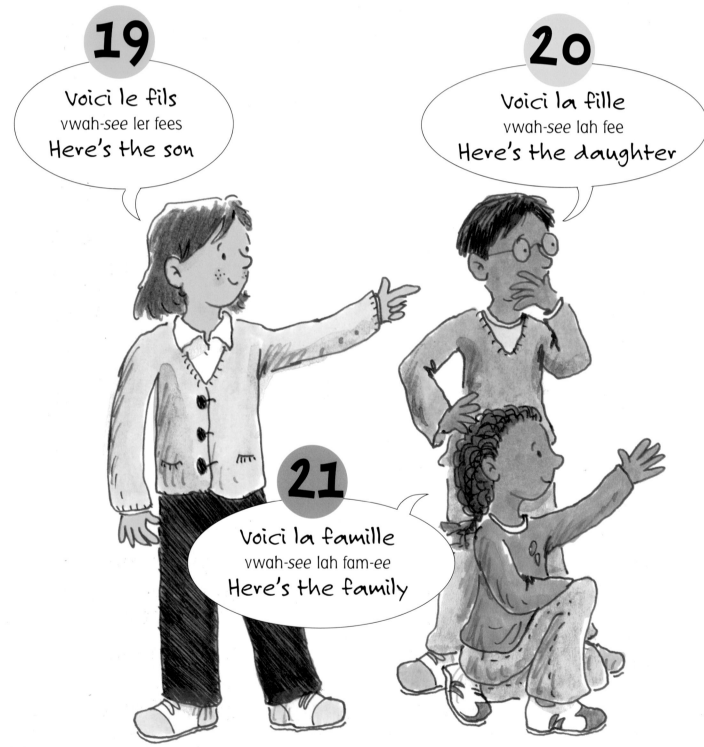

19

Voici le fils
vwah-*see* ler fees
Here's the son

20

Voici la fille
vwah-*see* lah fee
Here's the daughter

21

Voici la famille
vwah-*see* lah fam-*ee*
Here's the family

Words to Know

la mère/maman
lah mair/mam*oh*
mother/mum

le père/papa
ler pair/pa*pa*
father/dad

les parents
leh pah-*roh*
parents

la sœur
lah sir
sister

le frère
ler frair
brother

le bébé
ler beh-*beh*
baby

la grand-mère
lah groh-*mair*
grandmother

le grand-père
ler groh-*pair*
grandfather

J'aime...

Have a look at this picture and try to learn the French words for everything. Then choose four things you like and four you don't like. Practise saying if you like them or not by using the phrases **J'aime...** and **Je n'aime pas....** For example, **J'aime les fleurs** or **Je n'aime pas les moustiques**. Practise with a friend and take turns.

les chèvres
lay shevr
goats

les moustiques
lay *mooss*-teek
mosquitos

22

J'aime,...
shem
I like,...

23

Je n'aime pas,...
sh'nem pah
I don't like,...

la pluie
lah ploo-ee
rain

les lapins
lay lah-*pah*
rabbits

les fleurs
lay fler
flowers

les chats
lay shah
cats

le soleil
ler so*lay*
sun

les arbres
*l*ay *zar*-br'
trees

les canards
lay can-*ar*
ducks

les araignées
lay zaray-nee-*ay*
spiders

les cochons
*l*ay koh-*shoh*
pigs

les chiens
lay shee-*yah*
dogs

17

Où habites-tu?

The children in the pictures are telling us where they live.
Practise saying the phrases. Then cut out four pieces of paper
to cover speech bubbles 25-8 and number them from 1 to 4.
Ask a friend or adult to call out **un**, **deux**, **trois** or **quatre**
and say **Où habites-tu?** You have to try and remember
how to say where you live according to the scene
next to the number.

24

Où habites-tu?
oo ab-*eet* too
Where do you live?

25

J'habite une maison
sh'ab-*eet* oon meh-*zoh*
I live in a house

26

J'habite un appartement
sh'ab-*eet* ahn appa-ter-*moh*
I live in an apartment

Je voudrais...

Have some fun with this French shopping game for two or more people. Look at the shopping list and practise the words. The first player says **Je voudrais des pommes, s'il vous plaît** and then points at the next thing on the list, the strawberries, on the market stall. The next player has to add them to the phrase, saying **Je voudrais des pommes et des fraises, s'il vous plaît**. Each player adds another thing to the list. The winner is the first one to say the whole list correctly. Then you can shout **C'est tout, merci.**

29
Je voudrais...
sh' vood-*reh*
I would like...

30
S'il vous plaît
seel-voo-*pleh*
Please

31
C'est tout, merci
seh *too* mair-*see*
That's all, thanks

20

The Shopping List

des pommes
deh pom
(some) apples

des fraises
deh fraiz
(some) strawberries

des bananes
deh ban-*an*
(some) bananas

des raisins
deh ray-*zah*
(some) grapes

des carottes
deh kah-*rot*
(some) carrots

des pommes de terre
deh pom der tair
(some) potatoes

des tomates
deh tom-*at*
(some) tomatoes

de la salade
der lah sah-*lad*
(some) salad/lettuce

21

Un verre d'eau, s'il vous plaît

It's time to eat so have a go at asking for food and drink in French. You can ask a friend or adult to say **Qu'est-ce que tu veux?** All you need to do is choose something tasty from the menu and add **s'il vous plaît**. You might also like to say **J'ai faim** or **J'ai soif**.

32

Qu'est-ce que tu veux?
kesker too ver
What would you like?

33

J'ai faim
shay *fa*
I'm hungry

34

J'ai soif
shay *swaf*
I'm thirsty

Un verre d'eau, s'il vous plaît
ahn vair doh seel-voo-*pleh*
A glass of water, please

Menu/Le menu ler men-*yoo*

un jus d'orange
ahn joo dor-*ronsh*
an orange juice

un verre d'eau
ahn vair doh
a glass of water

un verre de lait
ahn vair der lay
a glass of milk

un morceau de gâteau
ahn morso der gat-*o*
a piece of cake

un yaourt
ahn yah-*oort*
a yogurt

des fruits
deh froo-ee
some fruit

du pain
dew pan
some bread

du jambon
dew shom*boh*
some ham

du fromage
dew from*ah-sh*
some cheese

des chips
deh sheep
some crisps

Qu'est-ce que tu veux faire?

You need two or more people to play this acting game.
Read the phrases and then cover them up. One of you
asks **Qu'est-ce que tu veux faire?** and acts out one
of the activities. The other player, or players, answer
Je veux… whatever they think the activity is.
Take it in turns to be the actor.

36

Qu'est-ce que tu veux faire?
kesker too ver *fair*
What do you want to do?

37

Je veux regarder la télé
sh' ver r'gar-*deh* lah teh-*leh*
I want to watch TV

24

38

Je veux jouer au football
sh' ver shoo-eh oh foot*bol*
I want to play football

39

Je veux faire du vélo
sh' ver *fair* doo *vay*lo
I want to cycle

40

Je veux nager
sh' ver nah-*shay*
I want to go swimming

Words to Know

Tu veux...?
too ver
Do you want to...?

Oui, je veux bien
wee sh' ver bee-*ah*
Yes, I'd like to

Non, merci
noh mair-*see*
No thanks

C'est de quelle couleur?

Here's a fun game to help you practise colours in French with your friends or family. You will need a die and some counters. When you land on a square all the other players shout **C'est de quelle couleur?** You say **Ma couleur préférée, c'est le rouge** or whatever colour you have landed on. If you get the answer wrong you miss a turn. Good luck!

41

C'est de quelle couleur?
seh de kel koo-*ler*
What colour is it?

42

Quelle est ta couleur préférée?
kel eh tah koo-*ler* prayfeh-*reh*
What's your favourite colour?

START

FINISH

Count in French
as you move
your counter.

43

Ma couleur préférée,
c'est le...
mah koo-*ler* prayfeh-*reh* seh ler...
My favourite colour is...

Colours/Les couleurs leh koo-*ler*

rouge	**vert**	**noir**	**orange**
rooshj	vair	nwah	oranshj
red	green	black	orange
bleu	**jaune**	**blanc**	**marron**
bl'	shown	bloh	mah-*roh*
blue	yellow	white	brown

Où vas-tu?

These children are all dressed for their holidays. See if you can match the right phrases to the children. Say **Où vas-tu?** and then choose the right answering phrase. Practise saying this out loud too. Check your answers on page 32.

44

Où vas-tu?
oo vah *too*
Where are you going?

45

Je vais à la plage
sh' vey ah lah plah-sh
I'm going to the beach

46

Je vais à la campagne
sh' vey ah lah kom-*pine*-y'
I'm going to the country

47

Je vais à la montagne
sh' vey ah lah mon-*tine*-y'
I'm going to the mountains

48

Je vais en ville
sh' vey ahn veel
I'm going to town

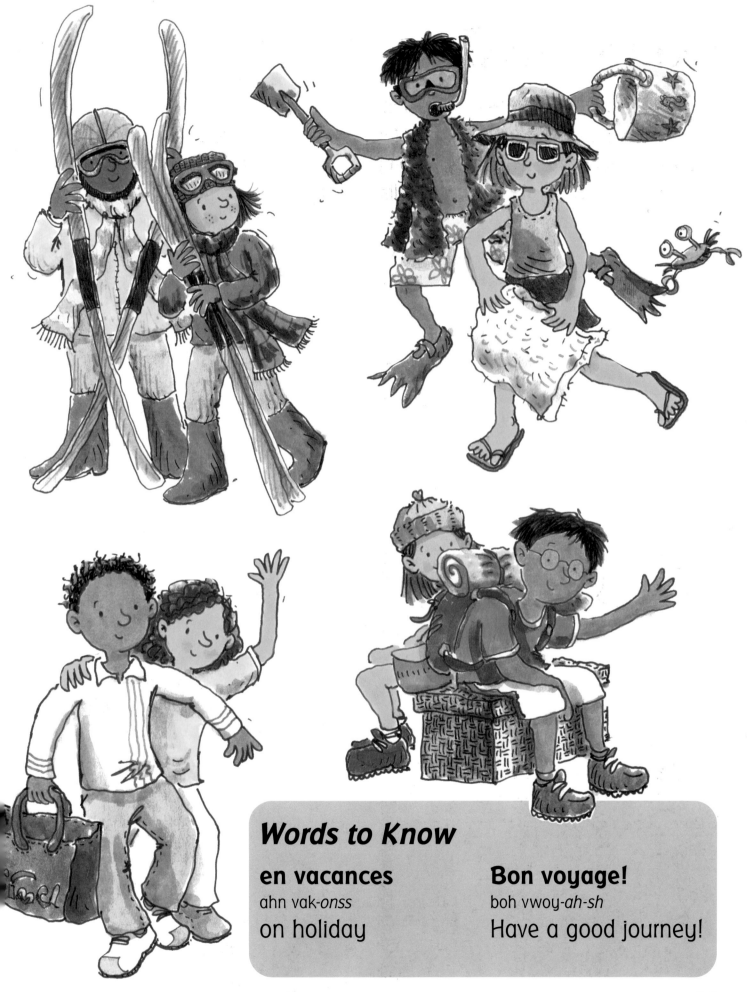

Words to Know

en vacances
ahn vak-*onss*
on holiday

Bon voyage!
boh vwoy-*ah-sh*
Have a good journey!

Je porte...

It is time to get dressed – in French! Have a look at the first picture and say **Je porte un petit pantalon**. Now look at the second picture and describe the difference in the trousers. Say **Je porte un grand pantalon**. Carry on describing the differences between the clothes on page 31. You'll need to use the **Words to Know** and have a look at the note about how to say 'big' and 'small' in French. You can check the answers on page 32.

Big or Small?
If the noun you are describing is a **le** (**un**) word,
you use **grand** or **petit**. If the noun is a **la** (**une**)
word, you use **grande** or **petite**. For example,
un grand manteau or **une grande robe**;
un petit manteau or **une petite robe**.

Words to Know

un pantalon	**un tee-shirt**	**une jupe**	**petit/petite**
ahn pantah-*loh*	ahn tee-*shairt*	oon shoop	p'tee/p'-teet
trousers	a T-shirt	a skirt	small
un manteau	**une casquette**	**un sweat**	**grand/grande**
ahn man-*to*	oon kas*ket*	ahn sweet	groh/grond
a coat	a cap	a sweatshirt	big

Solutions/Answers

Here are the answers to the activities on pages 2-3, 14-15, 28-9 and 30-1

pages 2-3

4 Bonne nuit
2 Au revoir
1 Bonjour
3 Bonsoir

pages 14-15

Voici la mère/maman

Voici le grand-père

Voici la fille/la sœur

Voici le fils/le frère

pages 28-9

47 Je vais à la montagne
45 Je vais à la plage
48 Je vais en ville
46 Je vais à la campagne

pages 30-1

Je porte un grand manteau

Je porte un grand tee-shirt

Je porte une grande jupe

Je porte un grand sweat

Je porte une grande casquette

Je porte un petit manteau

Je porte un petit tee-shirt

Je porte une petite jupe

Je porte un petit sweat

Je porte une petite casquette

50 phrases français/50 French Phrases

1 **Bonjour** Hello, good morning
2 **Au revoir** Goodbye
3 **Bonsoir** Good evening
4 **Bonne nuit** Goodnight
5 **Comment tu t'appelles?** What's your name?
6 **Je m'appelle…** My name is…
7 **Et toi?** And you?
8 **Quel âge as-tu?** How old are you?
9 **J'ai neuf ans** I am nine years old
10 **Bon anniversaire!** Happy birthday!
11 **Ça va?** How are you?
12 **Ça va bien, merci** I'm fine, thanks
13 **Ça ne va pas bien** I'm not so well
14 **Où est...?** Where is…?
15 **Voilà le/la…** Here is the…
16 **Encore une fois!** Try again!
17 **Qu'est-ce que c'est?** What is it?
18 **C'est un/une…** It's a…
19 **Voici le fils** Here's the son
20 **Voici la fille** Here's the daughter
21 **Voici la famille** Here's the family
22 **J'aime…** I like…
23 **Je n'aime pas…** I don't like…
24 **Où habites-tu?** Where do you live?
25 **J'habite une maison** I live in a house
26 **J'habite un appartement** I live in an apartment
27 **J'habite en ville** I live in town

28 **J'habite à la campagne** I live in the country
29 **Je voudrais…** I would like…
30 **S'il vous plaît** Please
31 **C'est tout, merci** That's all, thanks
32 **Qu'est-ce que tu veux?** What would you like?
33 **J'ai faim** I'm hungry
34 **J'ai soif** I'm thirsty
35 **Un verre d'eau, s'il vous plaît** A glass of water, please
36 **Qu'est-ce que tu veux faire?** What do you want to do?
37 **Je veux regarder la télé** I want to watch TV
38 **Je veux jouer au football** I want to play football
39 **Je veux faire du vélo** I want to cycle
40 **Je veux nager** I want to go swimming
41 **C'est de quelle couleur?** What colour is it?
42 **Quelle est ta couleur préférée?** What's your favourite colour?
43 **Ma couleur préférée, c'est le…** My favourite colour is…
44 **Où vas-tu?** Where are you going?
45 **Je vais à la plage** I'm going to the beach
46 **Je vais à la campagne** I'm going to the country
47 **Je vais à la montagne** I'm going to the mountains
48 **Je vais en ville** I'm going to town
49 **Je porte un petit pantalon** I'm wearing small trousers
50 **Je porte un grand pantalon** I'm wearing big trousers